T0353930

Stubby Dale:
Life is as good as you make it

SUZY LYNCH CUMMINGS

authorHOUSE

AuthorHouse™
1663 Liberty Drive
Bloomington, IN 47403
www.authorhouse.com
Phone: 833-262-8899

Published by AuthorHouse 11/04/2024

ISBN: 979-8-8230-3274-2 (sc)
ISBN: 979-8-8230-3273-5 (e)

Library of Congress Control Number: 2024917772

This book is dedicated to the Southeast Texas humane society in Beaumont Texas. Without them, I never would have connected with Stubby Dale. Charlotte Koch, contacted me, arranged the meeting and adoption. I had to rush to build a fence before I could bring him home, as they required. The rest is history. I am forever grateful for the people of the Humane Society in Beaumont., as they gave my sweet baby a warm place to wait for his forever home, as well as loving him, which was so very evident when he arrived. They are never forgotten.

My bed in Louisiana.

I AM STUBBY DALE CUMMINGS, A NATIVE Texan. I sort of know where the name Stubby began. Someone took my tail and it made sense to call me that. Life began for me one night on Highway I10 in Beaumont, Texas. Someone saw me. I don't remember anything before that. A very nice couple picked me up on their way home in the evening. I was a little red puppy without a tail, hungry, wet from rain and tired. I don't know how I lucked out but I just know I ended up at a nice warm shelter and I was fed, given water to drink and everyone thought I was extremely cute. Life was good. I didn't know any different. I was there for over a year. WE ran and played, ate and slept and occasionally someone would put me on a leash and we would go galavanting to festivals or just for a walk. Those were very special times. The caretakers were very nice, loving and took good care of us. They called themselves East Texas humane society. I was attached to a lady named Miss Charlotte Koch. She held on to me for a year until a softer spot could be found. They advertised for my forever home. I always knew something bigger than people and dogs looked after me and sort of "fought for me." I called him Big Dog. Humans write it backwards and call it GOD.

Big Dog put Miss Koch in my life so she could help me find a home and take care of me until.

Exodus 14:14 "The Lord himself will fight for you, Just stay calm."

"Big Dog always has my back if I stay calm."

Sometimes, people would come look at us and dogs would go off with people and never come back to the shelter. The caretakers told us that they were rescued which means adopted to a forever home...I was not worried. I prayed at night on my little bed that if it was a good thing, I would get a forever home. I wasn't sure so I just lived every day like it was all I had. During the year and a half that I lived in the shelter, I saw lots of dogs and sort of decided what I would do if I got out. "ADVENTURE AWAITS", I would think. I had dreams about who would choose me. I always awakened just hoping it was someone fun and adventuresome., not a dead beat that sat around and watched me.

My mama after I rescued her.

On my second Christmas at the shelter, they cleaned me up, put a Christmas collar on me and said we were going to Louisiana to meet someone named Suzy who was looking at me on a computer (Petfinder). She thought I was the prettiest dog she had ever seen. That was different because they said I was cute but still I hadn't found a forever home. Suzy kept seeing my picture and said she knew what I was like by just the video and pictures. They gave me a hamburger and French fries on the way and when I saw Suzy, I fell in love and knew she was my forever person.

Suzy told me on the way home to Louisiana, that I had a dad too. His name was Lewis. When we got home, Mama (Suzy) and Daddy (Lewis) took turns getting to fuss over me and love on me. I ate very well that night and they had a nice little bed on the floor-- even nicer than the shelter had for me. I jumped over it, crawled up on the bed in between them and my life changed forever that night. I was 1 1/2 years old and my life of fun, adventure and getting my way had just begun. Woof woof (Im home and happy). I could tell that Suzy and Lewis were just what I needed and had always prayed for. They were people ready to spoil me and a little naive which worked for me. Suzy had a special friend named Jimmy Dale and she loved the name, Dale for a middle name for me. Stubby Dale became my forever name. I had found my forever home. I looked up toward heaven and barked. Woof woof woof (Thank you Big Dog to answered prayers). Stubby Dale Cummings has just been launched.

Never did I feel bad about the time spent in a shelter where they took good care of me for over a year. I know all about love and faithfulness and those people were both.

Exodus 34:6. "I am slow to anger and filled with unfailing love and faithfulness"

"As long as there are treats and smiles, I'll be there"

Convincing my mom isn't always
easy. It can take a while.

Dogs don't have to search for their higher power. We are born with it. We were part of Gods creation from the beginning just as humans were. St. Francis of Assisi loved us way back before I was born in Texas. Humans spend their lifetime looking for the things we, dogs, are born with, Love, Humility, understanding forgiveness, happiness, adventure, self sufficiency and being able to "give back". Once I heard my DAD tell someone,: If you ever question a dogs forgiveness, lock a friend and a dog in the trunk of your car. When you let them out, which one is happy to forgive.??" It was a joke but, he made his point. Spell God backwards and what do you get?

Exodus 39:43 "He blessed them"

"Big Dog blesses all dogs."

Very soon, in my new home, Daddy took me to another place that looked like a shelter and called it day care. I loved it there because I could play all day, while Mama and Daddy worked. I got treats, played with other dogs and then Mama would pick me up and we would go have adventures. She took me everywhere and I barked and had fun no matter where we went. She didn't like that I always barked at people, so they enrolled me in manners classes. They had to go with me. A mean, sort of sad lady made up new rules for me and I had to not only quit barking so much but also not have treats unless I did something extra special. I went along with it knowing that after classes we would get back to normal at home. I knew Big Dog didn't go along with this. Some humans don't get it at all. Some people don't even have a dog. So, go figure!!!! My forever family gets it. My forever family even had a grandmother some of my life who lived in Denton, Texas. We got to go there and see her and she loved spoiling me.

She bought toys, which were fun and sweatshirts, which I tolerated for her.

Ruth 1:16 Wherever you go, I will go, Wherever you live, I will live, your people will be my people and my god, your GOD"

"I'll always be faithful to Big Dog in heaven"

Daddy took care of sick children at the hospital so when he went to do rounds, I got to go ride with him and sit in the truck while he went in. We did this every day. People would see us in the truck and laugh at me because he drove fast and I knew just how to lean with the turns. I had my own spot on his console. Other people and dogs sometimes had to sit in the back seat. No matter where I went or with whom, I rode the console.

Sometimes the kids at the hospital, would get to look out the window at me and talk about how cute I was. I pretended I didn't see them. Everyday life was good as I had food, water, other dogs, and people in the house. I had to get used to interlopers because my parents had friends and family. I usually liked them and they liked me but when I got tired of them getting all the attention, I would look at my mom and say woof woof woof (Lets go to bed so these nice people can go home.) It was special when people brought other dogs. I always felt a little sad if they had to sleep in a cage. I always freely and that is how it should be. Sometimes they would take me places where I couldn't jump on the furniture. Although not being allowed on the furniture, was wrong and hurtful, I did as I was told so I could stay and do whatever they were doing. When I couldn't change it, I tried to just accept the rules, stupid or not. Let go and let Big Dog.

Psalm 9:1. "I will praise you Lord with all my heart"

"I remember to pray even when I am not in a pinch"

My yard in Texas.

My daddy, Lewis.

I see no reason for loud, scary noises like thunder or fireworks. Im allergic to the noise. Im not afraid, even when it makes me shake. On my first New Years with Mama and Daddy, neighborhood kids shot fireworks all day. I had my allergy come on and Daddy took me out to do my business on a leash. I found It necessary to run off for the first time....I pulled out of my collar, left Daddy with the leash, and I had a three day adventure. While I was gone, I chased squirrels, ate road kill, drank from the Vermilion River and went swimming with alligators. My parents cried the whole three days I was gone. When I decided I was tired and hungry for my doggy bowl food, I went home. Everyone cried, we had a happy reunion. They bathed me and I slept for a long long time. They were on the phone telling everyone that I had been scared and had run from fireworks. They honestly believed it. Bless their hearts.!! Sometimes you just have to think like a dog and go with it. I can't think like a person because their thinking is messed up. It made them appreciate me a lot more when I returned home. So, I was to try my little disappearing act time and time again.

Jeremiah 29:11 I know the plans I have for you says the Lord…Plans for good and not disaster to give you a future and a hope"

"Big Dog knows what is going to happen way before I do"

One weekend, we were in Austin, staying in a motel. Mama took me out to do my business before breakfast. I found it necessary to break loose and take a joy run. My parents were not happy. They decided to go eat breakfast and leave me be. Well, I ran until I was tired, got back to the room and they had not even left water for me to drink after the run. I sat dutifully by the door and when they returned we pretended it didn't happen and went on about our day. I really like that about them both. Forgivness is easy for them. If they thought I did something wrong, they never let on. They laughed and said I was easier than kids anyway.

People are strange. They can't help it. My human brother is Yater. He is cool because he likes dogs. Once he had a friend named Rachel. He and Rachel had five dogs, Talk about fun!!! When we got together, it was usually a holiday with lots of food around. They knew how to get the people to keep the nibbles coming. I learned a lot from them.

One of my favorite lessons was how to push up against someone under the table until they sneaked us a piece of people food. They would lay their heads in peoples laps and act sweet. I didn't really like that part because it felt desperate but it worked when nothing else did. People always take turns slipping bites to us and never want the other people to know. That's because they try to act like they are listening to each other and they are really wishing they could just take a nap or come play with us. Isn't that stupid? Hide that you are doing a favor. Whatever.!! I guess they would want us to treat them the same way.

John 3:16 "Do unto others as you would have them do unto you"

"Treat all other dogs and some people the same"

Adventures make me smile.

One of Rachel and Yater's dog was named Deets. Rachel and Yater went their separate ways and I hadn't seen Deets in a long time. We were on the second floor of my grandmothers apartment, one Thanksgiving night. Mama said Rachel and Deets are here and opened the balcony door to look over. I got excited and flew through the rails of the balcony from the second story and landed, gently and beautifully, like a jet on a runway, It was a proud moment and the people all squealed and screamed like a bunch of scared cats. I just laughed at them and let them continue worrying about me. Of course I was fine. Life is only as exciting as you make it. Adventure is all part of it. I wish people could learn that from dogs. We all went back upstairs and had cake and ice cream. After all, Deets was there. He crossed rainbow bridge soon after that so I was thankful that he had that visit with me. It was a celebration. Dogs love celebrations. I did throw up a prayer of thanksgiving of my own to Big Dog. Im happy to be alive. Thank you Big Dog.

Another time at day care, I got a bite from a chow. Chows aren't playful with everyone. I guess I irritated him and he bit me. I had stitches and ignored him the rest of the time. I wasn't afraid of him, he just wasn't my type. The blessing in this was, it scared the day care workers and they sent him to a bigger group.

John 1:16. "From His abundance we have all received one gracious blessing after another."

"Count the good runs and be happy"

One of my favorite things to do is get in the car and travel. We did plenty of that in my early days. Mama, Daddy and I would go all over Texas to see friends and family. I knew to be a good boy. I would sit in the car while they went to eat and always got a doggy bag afterwards.

One time, it was too hot to sit in the car so they took me into the stock room at a restaurant and a kid watched me for a while. Another time, they paid the parking attendant to keep an eye on me. Humility is knowing someone is having to watch you to make sure you behave. The doggy bag made it ok. They knew I would forget at that point.

Matthew 6:34. "Don't worry about tomorrow."

"Every day is the same. Make it the best"

One time they left me in the car while they ran into the grocery store. The weather was great. They took a little longer than I wanted them to. I usually timed them but this time they were slow, so I climbed out the window and went into the store to find them. I stepped on a mat and the door sprung wide open. I had never seen anything like that. I sprinted through the store until I found them. That was a huge surprise for them. Daddy picked me up and took me out. That is the only grocery store visit I've gotten to make. Before I found my parents inside the store, I heard someone ask "Is that Stubby?" So much for being discreet. Every store doesn't welcome me, but when they do I always go in. I love restaurants that have patios. Some have treats and water bowls. Life Is meaningful and I feel appreciated more when this happens. Im so glad IM not afraid to take risks. Life is way too short, they say but after all I am 18 years old, so I don't know if that makes sense. Ive just heard it.

Matthew 10:31 "Don't be afraid"

One day, I was hanging out the window of the car in our neighborhood. I saw a squirrel and couldn't resist. I flew out of the window to chase it but landed wrong in the street. I was a bloody mess. The vet sewed me up and I was as good as new. It worried my parents but everything did at times. I couldn't change my whole life because they worried. If I lived life to please everyone, I would not have been the Stubby Dale, they adopted. Yater always says, "Bubby is living his best life". Yes I am. IM sort of famous. People who I've met don't usually forget me. Once at the drive through bank, the teller said "is that "Stubby Dale". Mom was very surprised and said yes. She had known hIm at the day care and was now a bank teller. I know, I spread joy and love everywhere I go. I don't mean to but it happens. And those who know better, slip me a treat in the rolling container. Just out spreading joy to those who care is so much fun. OH, and getting a treat rocks too.

Mark 16:15 "Go into all the world and preach the good news to everyone"

"One of my dog jobs is to spread joy"

Once in Austin, my mom decided to run the turkey trot race. She kept saying, I'll take Stubby but if he doesn't want to run the entire race Ill just walk some. When I heard that, I was determined. WHAT?? AS if I would be the one to quit. So, the race started and I took off in a sprint. We ran the five miles faster than mom ever had. When we crossed the finish line Dad gave us water and we went home. That taught them to NEVER doubt my activity level.

So far, the Episcopal Church has blessed me 17 times. My parents always thought I would act nicer and be loved more by neighbors and others (who don't understand me) if I would get blessed on St. Francis of Assisi Day. That is when St, Francis is celebrated in our church. He loved all creatures. I agree with him about all but cats. Cats are bothersome and sometimes they show up with cats to be blessed at church on that day. They make stupid noises and have to be kept in cages so they can't bother the rest of us.

Last year, the church organist brought a turtle, named Herman who lives in his own custom built home. He rocked. He was fun and minded his own business. I sniffed around on him and he didn't care at all. All the other pets are fun and act nice at church. Just not the cats. At the end, they give us treats but the cats can't have them. I felt like St. Francis probably wouldn't have blessed cats except he had to so he could stay a Saint. I heard God told him "just include them, they know not what they do". Speaking of cats, once my dad was walking me and all I did was look in one of those pipes that run in a ditch. To my surprise, a stupid cat was hiding, waiting for me. Just as I saw him, he slapped me in the head for nothing. I couldn't even chase him. My dad pulled me back and treated me like a big sissy who couldn't defend himself. That was the worst thing he ever did to me. It was just wrong on so many levels. The cat could roam free and I was on a leash being lead around. UGH! Where is Big Dog when someone let the cats out.

Romans 8:31. "If God is for us, who can ever be against us?"

If Big dog is for us, who is against us?"

I hope she stops at Sonic, oops too late,
maybe starbucks NOPE, lets just go home.

My Dad got a disease where he could't remember stuff. They had nurses come in and take care of him all day and Yater and I watched him all night so Mama could sleep. That was cool because between Yater and the ladies that watched my dad, they fixed me up with treats and all I did was hang out and ask for more. I was doing just fine, better than fine, until the day my vet, saw me walking down the street on a leash with my mama.

Miss Angie was my Louisiana vet and I love her. She loved me but when she saw me from behind, she said I had gotten fat. So, that ruined everything. They quit giving me treats. I had to eat green beans and dog food. NO TREATS. I really resented my parents who could have ignored her, But later I slimmed back down and they gave me treats again, just not as many. Dad was a great dad. Everyone loved him, especially Mom. She was sad when he died and so was I. But we cuddled a lot and I didn't mind doing that to help her get happy again. My mom's boss said, "When I die, I want to come back as

Stubby". it IS a good life. When my dad died, he went to human heaven. I prayed it was as good as over the rainbow bridge and I know prayers work so I know he is happy, joyous and free. I really believe Big Dog helped me get through it. Acts 27:25." I believe God."

"I believe in Big Dog"
(the God of my understanding)

Each year Mama and I walked in the parade for dogs. Krewe des chin. We were members. You had to be a dog to be a crew member and it had to be Mardi Gras season which I LOVED. Everyone stayed home all week and went to parades and had company and left us alone. On the day of OUR parade, Mama dressed me in Mardi Gras clothes and we walked a loop downtown. She threw candy and I got to sniff a bunch of other dogs and get doggy treats. The doggy parade in 2015 was the day after my dad died. We were sitting there feeling sad and mama got up and dressed us and we went downtown and walked in the parade. It was a special day. People clapped for me and I got more treats because they were proud of us for showing up.

One time we were driving to Texas from Louisiana. I was sitting up on my console when the car went out. It just stopped. Mama called AAA and they said it would be a while. We waited and I ate beef jerky until I was almost sick. It was sort of hot so we sat in the AC in a service station pretty close to where we broke down. When the guy from AAA came, he brought a tow truck. He said mama could ride with him but I would have to sit in the towing car. It was fine with me. What a great adventure. People thought I was driving. I balanced myself up on the console and pretended to drive. Right after we started, we stopped and the people got out of the truck. Mama was crying and the tow guy was fussing and finally they put me in the cab of the truck with them. It wasn't as much fun but it was a lot better than listening to a bunch of bellyaching about where I sat. That was just another difference in people and dogs.

There was another time when mama had surgery and Yater came to visit. While she was sitting in the bed, I found and killed a squirrel. When I brought it through the doggy door, even Yater wasn't happy and he usually didn't get too excited. He made me turn around and take it out. No one was happy and I felt terrible, not because I killed and brought it in but because they acted unappreciative. Another time when Mama was at her computer, I found a dead squirrel in the yard. This time something else killed it. When I brought it in, I just wanted to nibble on it while she stayed on the computer. I got by with it for only a few minutes. She looked down and kicked us out the front door. This is one time I didn't run off but sat by the door until she sorted it all out in her head and let me back in. HOWEVER; I had to have a bath and have my teeth brushed. The rest of the night I questioned if it was worth it. People!!!

Once mom and I had a bad experience. We were walking in Tyler Texas and four pit bulls attacked us. I had to go for help. I ran to a ladies door and banged on it until she came. While I was gone, another lady who was a nurse was going home from work. She came up honking and finally they let go of my mom. I really was glad they all helped her. I could have taken them on all alone, but saw no reason to when I could go get help. I know they were a little afraid of me because they let go when I was seen coming back. Mama got some bruises and pretty bad bites but nothing like what would have happened if I had gotten hold of them. I think they knew that. We went to Yaters house and mama and I cuddled all night because thats one of my jobs as her watchdog.

Acts 15:11 "We are all saved the same way, by the undeserved grace of Lord Jesus"

"Grace is a doggy treat when you return from a fun run off the leash."

Mama retired a few years after Dad died. She decided we were going back to Texas. We had been in Louisiana for a long time. We went to visit and we both liked Granbury a lot. It had good smells, nice people water bowls outside of many places of business and we found a new day care where I could go play. Every day close to our house, we see a Llama, some cows, a goat farm and some longhorns. The sun is out a lot and it isn't humid so I don't stink as bad as I did, in Louisiana, my mom says. I do not miss the rain or the thunder. It doesn't do a lot of that in

Granbury and I get to see Dinky, my little neice, Yater and Anita (Dinkys parents) more because we live closer.

Acts 17:28 "In Him we Live and move and exist."

"Big Dog sets the example for how I live. He's in my dreams"

From L to R, Dinky Lynch, Uncle Yater Lynch and yours truly dressed for game day Hook em Horns!!

Notice the tight leash. I was oh,
so close but no cigar.

I mentioned that I had jumped out of a car, over a second story balcony, and. I even awakened a possum who wanted to fight, but no vet has ever been able to explain why I have a bullet in my x-rays. (BB) I will not reveal that at this point. All I will say about that is, to tell about it would scare my mom. She doesn't need to know everything.

2 Timothy 1:7 "God has not given us spirit of fear and timidity but of power, love, and self discipline."

"I will live to be a better dog"

My love life is really no ones business but I have had one. I like bitches that are sort of rough, like to bark a lot and run. But then some girl dogs are just beautiful, well groomed, polite and attractive, I can't refuse them but you can't count on them for a good time. They are full of drama, close to their parents and blame me for stuff that isn't my fault. I much prefer not getting serious about anyone and I like just hanging out with dogs that my mom knows.

My little niece, Dinky girl is fun because she barks a lot and goes outside with me and hides from our parents. However, she has girl feet and gets on my nerves when she is picky or doesn't ask for enough treats. She doesn't have a bullet inside her and she doesn't take enough risks in my opinion but I love her anyway. I taught her to look down drain pipes and she got bit on the nose by a snake twice. Some just can't handle it. She got pampered and I got blamed.

Mama and me in Kerville, Texas. Hiking on
a very cold day. I love the hill country.

Once, visiting Dinky, Yater and Anita in Tyler, Yater took me over to Anitas house. I saw fit to run out a cracked, open door. It might have been my favorite run, and Ive had plenty. It definitely got to everyone a little more. The two of them chased me under a bridge, through a drainage area, into a creek and I smelled that Anita had a piece of chicken to bribe me with. This wasn't my first Rodeo. I grabbed it out of her hand and took off even faster. I usually wind down with these things when the adults tire of chasing me or run out of food, whichever comes first. We went back to Anitas had "good boy" treats and went home. Life is what you make it.

1 corinthians 16:14 "Do everything with Love."

"Do everything with puppy love"

The play bow gets lots of attention if
you do it at the right time. (not before
meals or when anyone is mad)

One time we went to Kerville so we could hike. There was a nice mountain that we wanted to climb. No dogs were allowed grrrrr but it was January and not crowded and did I mention we don't like rules? If mama had followed the rules I never would have achieved the goal. The trail was called (Enchanted rock). We took water and treats with us and had a great day. We reached the top and felt proud.

Mom is athletic so when I came to her in 2007, we walked 5 miles a day for years. We both slowed down a bit in 2021 when we moved to Granbury, texas. She still walks but on the long walks she leaves me at home because I rest more since Im older. I cannot see or hear but I can still smell and know what is going on. We go on short walks every day.

2 corinthians 5:7. "We live by believing and not by seeing"

"We live my sniffing and believing in our Big dog"

This is one of those times you have to
please your mom. I won an ugly sweater
contest. OMG battery operated lights
and tinsel. Talk about embarrassing!!!!

I have a statement to make to all dogs of any age and, especially older ones so listen up!!. Some of us had a few hard days, other days were calming, fun or fulfilling. We have all had good times. Ive shared a few. I know my life isn't going to be a whole lot longer. Dogs are not stupid and I'm smarter than most. Humans need to be comforted when our end gets near. I don't want to lay around and hurt and be unexcited about my treats and my walks if that ever happens. I am not saying Im ready but I will be if Im ever sick or in pain. I do NOT mind crossing rainbow bridge when that day comes. From what I hear, its one adventure after another just like our dreams are. Its bonding with other dogs and being loved eternally. I wasn't blessed 17 times for nothing. When its my turn, Ill just say "Im coming home over the rainbow bridge baby and Im looking forward to eternal life." Big Dog can always use a new and perfect angel and when my work is done on earth, let me go with dignity and grace. Life is as good as you make it.

Philippians 4:4 "Always be full of joy in the Lord. Again, I say rejoice"

And for those who are left behind:

Genesis 9:16 "When I see a rainbow in the clouds, I will remember the eternal covenant between God and every living creature on earth."

Until we meet again, remember that Life is as good as you make it.

Always time for a prayer to
thank Big Dog for my life.

About the Author

Suzy Lynch Cummings grew up in Cleburne, Texas. Her entire family loved dogs, cars, horses and cows.

After graduating from Cleburne Highschool, University Of Texas and University of Louisiana, she settled into a family and career in Education. She loved teaching creative writing, integrated with music and Art.

Suzy does not consider herself an author but loves to journal and put creativity into it to make a fun read. She wrote Oh Goodness, Oh Gracious, a children's book about "doing the right thing" as well as several articles and stories used in educating children.

She now is retired and lives in Granbury, Texas with Stubby Dale. They both enjoy traveling, walking, going on drives, doggy parks and exploring. Suzy plays Saxaphone, reads, plays tournament bridge and is active at her Episcopal church.

She thinks every household should make room for a pet.